What couples are saying about
Grandpa Does Grandma:

"It's about time someone shared the realities and possibilities of senior sex."

"Grandpa doesn't understand Grandma's continuing need for sex anymore than Grandpa understands Grandma's need for ongoing affection. Finally, Phil addresses the challenge."

"Parker must have been hiding in my bedroom when he wrote Grandpa Does Grandma. What he says really works."

"Grandpa Does Grandma gave me confidence to experiment with my wife."

"Phil Parker takes a serious subject and presents it in a light hearted manner that makes it easy to read without losing his message."

"I loved participating in your focus group and getting a insider's peek at the book. Phil, this is terrific."

"Originally I thought this book would be TMI, to much information. After reading a few excerpts I laughed and learned a lot. Thanks."

"The illustrations in your book are fabulous and a great addition to great content."

"It doesn't matter if you're young or old, Grandpa Does Grandma gives you the green light to keep sex going at any age."

To Pat & Chuck,
May you both enjoy a
long life together!
Phil

Grandpa Does Grandma©
The ABCs of Senior Sex

by
Phil Parker

Phil Parker

Copyright: 2015 by Phil Parker
Cover Design by: Beyond Business Solutions, LLC
Illustrations by: Rafael D. Nazario
Photography by: Howard Silverman
Edited by: Cindy Elsberry
Printed by: Publishers' Graphics, LLC
Website: www.GrandpaDoesGrandma.com
by Beyond Business Solutions, LLC

ISBN-13: 978-0-9724061-6-1
ISBN-10: 0-9724061-6-6

Published by:

Lilli Publishing
3151 Stillhouse Creek Drive, SE
Apartment 4423
Atlanta, GA 30339

DEDICATION

This book is dedicated to all the
grandpas and grandmas that are still doing it.

To all their children who refuse to believe that
their parents ever did it.

To the younger generation who hope
they can keep on doing it.

And, last, but not least:
To all who say, "T.M.I." (Too Much Information).

SPECIAL DEDICATION

I also dedicate this book to my in-laws,
Lillian and Robert Renert, who shared a loving,
nurturing and intimate marriage for over 60 years.

A Special Message from Karen Giblin

Sex can be pleasurable, no matter what your age!! One very important ingredient to achieving good sex is communication. Changes do occur as a result of normal aging in both men and women. This may cause a loss of sexual interest, especially if problems are not openly identified, discussed and treated.

Phil Parker stresses the importance of good communication while never underestimating the value of caressing, kissing, and understanding his wife's (Grandma) feelings. He's kept that magical spark in his relationship proving that it is possible to keep sex and passion alive in a long-term and also senior relationship.

Bonnie and Phil Parker are seniors. They are satisfied in bed, and satisfied in life!!! *Grandpa Does Grandma* is a landmark book; it will bring a smile to the faces of all people who are over the age of sixty. With sexual exuberance, Phil clearly demonstrates that excitement and enthusiasm can last forever.

This book offers insightful A-Z advice, solutions and tantalizing tips to seniors - encouraging couples that the sexual, passionate feelings they had when they were young can be maintained at any age. It is highly entertaining, informative, providing wit, wisdom, as well as a positive spin to sex in one's golden years. *Grandpa Does Grandma* offers steamy suggestions that certainly will supercharge the sex lives of seniors!!!

Karen Giblin
Founder/President
Red Hot Mamas Menopause Programs

ACKNOWLEDGEMENTS

As with writing any book, when asked, there are always individuals who are willing to share their time and expertise about a subject on which they are passionate or have experienced first hand. When I first considered my subject matter, I was concerned that not enough of my peer group (seniors) would step up to the plate to share their points of view. Imagine my surprise and delight when both men and women were equally willing to participate in several focus groups. Quite frankly, their ideas, experiences, creativity, openness and edgy feedback left me speechless.

Here's what I learned: Men and women differ significantly on their sexual points of view. While men are quick to describe sex as a physical activity, women, on the other hand, consider sex from an emotional perspective. The challenge that presented itself was, "How to write this book in a way that acknowledges both genders?"

I promised all the individuals that participated in this venture complete anonymity. They know who they are, how much their input helped me and how much I appreciate each of them.

We laughed, we shocked each other and we reveled in the fact that, as seniors we could talk openly about our sexual adventures or misadventures.

Most surprising of all were the women who conjured up unbelievable fantasy names for their spouse's/partner's private parts. Even at my age, I was shocked by their ideas and comments!

A special thanks goes to my brother, Bruce, whose creativity, insights and bizarre sense of humor contributed to this book.

And, to Suzanne and Howard Silverman and Chris and Dave Adams I extend my heartfelt gratitude for their continuing support and encouragement.

Of course, I owe a debt of gratitude to Grandma for being an incredible partner in all aspects of our marriage and for her understanding and willingness to indulge me in this project.

OVERVIEW

Grandpa Does Grandma: The ABCs of Senior Sex is a sexual romp through the alphabet and about a sexual sunrise in our golden years. It's about acknowledging and confirming that we're never too old to enjoy our bodies and the pleasure we derive from exploring and fulfilling one another. It's coming to the realization that as we age, intercourse and orgasm have become less important in our quest for sexual gratification, and that the absence of genital sex is not necessarily a tragic outcome. ***Grandpa Does Grandma*** is about reveling in what we've earned in respect, perseverance and taking pride in what we've accomplished by living well.

In doing research for ***Grandpa Does Grandma***, I spent considerable time browsing in the relationship/sexuality section and the magazine section of the bookstore. It was obvious that most sex books focus on positions, frequency and orgasms. How unrealistic! Naked pictures of brushed, lean and youthful bodies are a poor representation for those of us that have aged gracefully, can no longer contort our bodies as they would suggest and at this stage in our lives have more diverse activities than focusing on unrealistic sex.

As I thumbed through the many magazines that profess to show you how to enjoy more sex, better sex and orgasmic sex, one particular article stood out. It was entitled, "More Sex – Better Sex." Its wisdom claimed men are like microwaves and women are like slow cookers. Here are two other examples. In one publication I was offered "a beach ready body in 14 days" which is hardly attainable for a grandpa of 70. The other guaranteed to teach me how to "turn her on" every time. If I haven't figured it out by now, I'm probably slightly behind the curve.

It seems to me that the so-called experts and image makers measure us in terms of the way we look, what designer clothes we wear, and how many times a week we have sex. Who really cares? The magazines go on and on. Can we really measure up to what the "image makers" claim should be our goal? Of course not! It's not realistic and in most cases not possible.

Set yourself free from the expectations of others and begin to follow the expectations you establish for yourself. Life is not about comparing yourself to others. Aging is about deciding what is best for you and being happy with your choices.

The next time you browse the magazine section of your local bookstore, avoid the hype and promises of becoming a better you. You are great the way you are. So, simply smile, pat your self on the back and tell yourself...**I already measure up!**

There you have it. Whatever you learn and whatever you are willing to do to enrich, strengthen, and improve love and your love life, my hope for you is to have many rewarding years ahead to love, honor, and nurture each other. **Remember: Grandma can do Grandpa too!**

INTRODUCTION

Not long ago at my local Barnes & Noble bookstore where I usually begin each day with a few friends over coffee, a young female employee in her early 20s with whom I exchange morning pleasantries asked how old I was. "Going on 70," I replied, waiting for her to compliment me on how young and buff I looked. Instead, she hit me with the following question: "Now that you're almost 70 and you don't have sex anymore, what do you do for excitement?" She was serious! I quickly informed her that I "still have lead in my pencil," gave her a wink, and went about my business.

However, in the weeks that followed, her comments got me thinking. When I was in middle school and the thought of my parents having sex, who were then in their "old" forties, grossed me out. Even when I became a young adult, the idea of my mom and dad *"doing it"* was difficult to imagine. Let's face it, thinking about their parents engaging in *any* kind of sex freaks out most children.

Sexual mores and attitudes have become more liberal in our culture over the past few decades. The idea that men and women in their 60s, 70s and older continue to have fun, be passionate, and enjoy exciting, fulfilling, loving and aggressive sex, is still hard for many to imagine, as my young friend at the book store will attest. Sadly, this may also be true for "seniors," a platitude for older Americans, and this book was also written for them.

The reason for this gap between perception and reality is, in part, because ours is a culture of youth. Fortunately, this too, is changing. We are living and working longer, have a better understanding of the importance of exercise and the need to eat healthy, all of which is beginning to change our biological clocks.

George Burns, the beloved entertainer who was still going strong at 100 years of age said, "Everything that goes up first must come down. But there comes a time when not everything that's down can come up." We know this is not necessarily true for the young or the old because former Senator Bob Dole told us about Viagra® in his prime time television commercial.

There are 77 million baby boomers who are now 64 years of age. Don't think for a second that when you hear loud booming sounds in the sky that it's only thunder. It may be the bed boards banging as America's seniors enjoy a healthy, warm and active sex life.

As I approach my 70th birthday, sex is still important and Grandma and I enjoy a very active and healthy sex life. Being empty-nesters helps.

In an article in USA TODAY dated December 4, 2008, lead author Sara Gorchoff said; "The empty nest isn't a panacea that's making everything in their lives better, but it does have a specific impact on having better marriages because women are enjoying time with their partners more after the kids are gone." Gorchoff further states, "That even though marital satisfaction increased, overall life satisfaction did not."

I believe sexual energy is more a function of health rather than age. This wonderful intimacy spills over into our leisure activities, our work and our relationships with friends. Due to changing and challenging times, many seniors are working longer, which further emphasizes the changing sociality of aging and senior sexuality.

Sexual change is more difficult than changing jobs. When it comes to sex in this country, there are a lot of taboos. We need to change our attitudes towards sexuality as we age.

There seems to be a perceptual and emotional gap between young and old regarding sexual vitality and sexual expression, which, in itself, is misguided. Don't judge me just because I have wrinkled skin, grey hairs or no hair at all. Senior sex can be energetic, thrilling, sensual, disturbing and sometimes just plain weird.

All of us have many unspoken feelings about our real or perceived sexual inadequacies. What better time to experiment?

A 2007 study of 3,000 adults published in the *New England Journal of Medicine* found that half the people aged 65-74 and a quarter of those ages 75 to 85 reported being sexually active. (Defined as "any mutually voluntary activity with another person that involves sexual contact whether or not intercourse or orgasm occurs.") "A substantial number of men and women engage in vaginal intercourse, oral sex and masturbation even in the eighth and ninth decades of life," the study's authors concluded.

I predict that before long the next version of Carrie Bradshaw and her friends in "Sex and the City" will take place in an upscale independent living retirement community, and that Mr. Big will be a tall, athletic hunk who celebrated his last birthday at 100.

In closing, ***Grandpa Does Grandma*** was written with a serious underlying purpose and hopefully enjoyed as a light hearted, tongue in cheek, and somewhat edgy book. Its focus is to encourage the renewal of sexual intimacy for men and women who, upon becoming seniors, for whatever reasons have lost this need or desire and to provide them with suggestions on how to get their groove back.

For the younger generation, ***Grandpa Does Grandma*** provides new insights as to what is possible. Human touch is essential in order to flourish emotionally and physically at any age. For readers who have not broken stride in their sex life, these pages may bring a telltale smile or, better yet, teach a few old dogs some new tricks!

The ABCs of Senior Sex

Grandpa Does Grandma

The ABCs of Senior Sex

A

"I blame my mother for my poor sex life. All she told me was, 'the man goes on top and the woman underneath'. For three years my husband and I slept on bunk beds."
Joan Rivers

Always be grateful and always be ready. Show affection. Affection is not a sign of weakness but rather a sign of strength. Being affectionate, thoughtful and kind will spill into your sex life. Consider this mantra: Anytime, anywhere, in any way and in any place. Be willing to participate in early morning sex, mid-afternoon sex or middle of the night sex. As seniors, we are often at home during the day. Make yourself accessible to your partner's sexual desires. Senior sex doesn't always have to take place in a darkened or dimly lit bedroom. Make creativity your goal and eliminate the agony of anticipation.

Being aggressive is not necessarily the man's role. Many men like aggressive women! Be authentic...in your words and actions.

Andy Rooney said, "Men wake up in the morning aroused. We can't help it. We just wake up and want you. The women are thinking, 'How can you want me the way I look in the morning?' It's because we can't see you. We have no blood anywhere near our optic nerve." So why not consider arousing him by taking his morning erection in your hand, that is, if he still stands tall in the morning.

Let's face it. We often have some free time on our hands during the day. We may use this opportunity to putter around the house or garden or we can take advantage of that time and engage in an afternoon delight.

Note: The Centers for Disease Control and Prevention reported that AIDS cases among Americans over 50 quintupled since 1995.

Seniors, no longer concerned about preventing pregnancy, are one-sixth as likely to use condoms and one-fifth as likely to get tested for HIV as their younger peers, according to a Center for AIDS Prevention study.

ON THE SOFTER SIDE:

Appreciation – It's clear to me that the more men express gratitude to their partners, the more loving and willing women are to be sexual.

It seems that when women feel accepted for who they are, their changing bodies and aging in general, the more open minded and willing they become.

Women reported they respond to adoration, to being told they are attractive and hence can become very assertive when conditions are to their liking! So men, here's the lesson: appeal to what appeals to them! Authenticity! Be authentic with each other. What you see is what you get. Acknowledge your partner! Let him/her know exactly what you're thinking and how you feel about them.

Grandpa Does Grandma

B

"Senior sex is not like banking;
There is no penalty for early withdrawal."

Unknown

At this point in our lives we should all be skilled in the basic intercourse positions. As a reminder they are as follows; (1) Man on top (missionary position), (2) Woman on top, (3) Rear entry, (4) Side by Side (spooning) (5) Sitting and (6) Standing.

Begin each day with a few minutes of cuddling before you get out of bed. Grandpa can tell Grandma how nice it feels to be close to her and Grandma can do the same by telling Grandpa how wonderful it is to enjoy some early morning closeness as well.

Don't be a BHOF, i.e., a Bald Headed Old Fart! Be ready. As we age we tend to slow down and our availability and opportunities for sexual intimacy may decrease.

When presented with the opportunity, make no excuses! Take your Viagra® and keep the KY jelly close at hand.

Never refuse an offer from your partner. Engage in bedtime chatter. It will bring you closer.

Let me mention breasts briefly. Please recognize that grandma's large but aging breasts, i.e., cupid's kettledrums, may be a little fuller and a little lower but nonetheless can still provide excitement.

Bragging is not recommended. It's the younger generation that brags; the senior generation boasts!

ON THE SOFTER SIDE:

The skin is the largest organ of the body. There have been many books written about tactile experience, i.e. human touch. A woman's body is a sexual wonderland. Women simply love to be touched, to be treated gently and to feel a man's tenderness. Women love back rubs. There's something about touching her body, including her shoulders, buttocks, the inside of her thighs, and the bottom of her feet that can arouse her libido.

Bathe together. Call it foreplay. Call it "meeting your partner where she is." Call it whatever you want. Just do it!

Being heard. We've all heard this before! Are you listening? Did you hear me? Can you stop what you're doing while I'm talking? Women need conversation. They need acknowledgment and reassurance.

Hey, if that's what they want, and you can offer it, why not? That's how you will (hopefully) get what YOU want. Got the picture?

C

"My favorite color is Flesh."

Phil Parker

Condoms are no longer required unless you're playing the field with different partners, some of who may still be fertile. Let's face it, as men get older their women tend to get younger. Also, if you are sexually active with many partners, you run the risk of STDs (that's Sexually Transmitted Diseases for those of you who don't know). Make sure that "Captain Winkie" has a hat on. Keep some colored cloths close to your bed. They work a lot better then Kleenex® and are particularly useful for women who don't swallow during oral sex. Recognize that only in the movies or on TV is there no mess after an orgasmic senior sexual romp.

Consideration for Grandma's needs is important. Compliment her willingness to engage in some, shall we say, unusual sexual activities. Tune in to Grandma and whatever turns her on. Most men don't have a clue that women are complex sexual creatures capable of enormous sexual pleasure under the right set of circumstances.

ON THE SOFTER SIDE:

Caring. "OK!" You're thinking, "of course I care about Grandma. Of course I love her." The sixty-four thousand dollar question is: Does Grandma know how much you care about her and love her? Casual caresses also work wonders. Cater to her needs. Put the cap back on the toothpaste, replace the toilet paper when needed and most importantly, don't forget to put the toilet seat down.

I am connected emotionally, physically, sexually and spiritually with Grandma. Commitment is the glue that bonds us together.

Constant communication! We communicate our love for each other several times a day whether verbal or written. We enjoy being with each other. There is no person I would rather spend my time with than my wife. Simply stated, I totally respect, support and love Grandma.

Do you really communicate or do you simply assume she knows what you are thinking and feeling?

If you're saying to yourself, "We've been together forever, so of course she knows how much I love her," it's simply not enough. Talk to her! Tell her! Reassure her!

Have the confidence and courage to be an open book. Why not cuddle in a recliner built for two? If you don't have one, it would be a great purchase! Think about the fun of staying toasty warm, playing under the covers and arousing one another. My point is that women want, deserve and need connection. Increased connection can lead to increased sexual activity.

Don't forget candlelight. I can't say enough about the effect of candles. Even aging bodies look good under their warm glow. Keep one by that recliner built for two, on the nightstand or anywhere you think you can kindle romance. Don't forget something so simple to implement! Be certain to take candles with you when vacationing to set the stage for your candlelit lovemaking. There's something special about making love in a strange bed in strange surroundings away from our daily routine.

Grandpa Does Grandma

D

"The mirror over my bed reads:
Objects appear larger than they are."

Gary Shandling

Different positions can be tricky. Visit your local Barnes & Noble bookstore for books on the subject. You'll be shocked at the number of innovative positions you are not aware of or have not tried. The Kama Sutra, a book about sexual energy and positions, can be helpful. I was surprised at the number of positions I had not attempted. Be careful but be cautious. We don't want to keep the chiropractors busy. Be a dreamer! Think up some positions or activities that you haven't experienced before. We all know that men have a difficult time asking for directions let alone following them. Bed is the one place where men are the most willing to take directions and do what you tell them to do. Show him pictures, diagrams or books. It may take some concerted effort to get your message across.

ON THE SOFTER SIDE:

Sometimes I think men are delusional when we believe we can make our partners desire us just because we desire them! It all comes down to the same thing.

What are we doing to demonstrate love so that our partner will want to make love? Are we acknowledging her? Are we being kind, tender and appreciative?

Do we, as men, set the stage with our partner so that intimacy becomes the natural result of our behavior? If not? Why not?

Have you noticed how easily women become distracted? Even in their later years, it seems there is always something a woman must do to feel productive. If, for whatever reason she doesn't feel productive or valued, you'd better think of how you can turn her self-talk around. If a woman is pre-occupied, you don't stand a prayer when it comes to 'having sex'!

Consider making love during daylight. Yes, that's right. In the middle of the day! You're retired, aren't you? So, why wait until nighttime for the right time? The fact is that whether morning, noon, or night, the time is always right!

E

*"When two people love each other, every day is
Thanksgiving and every night is New Years Eve."*
Abigail Van Buren

I have always had great enthusiasm for the female body. Since
my days as a detail man for Ortho Pharmaceutical Corporation,
(the birth control division of Johnson & Johnson), I have been in
awe when in the presence of the naked female form. According
to **Sex Secrets of Escorts** by Veronica Monet, "...many men
consider female genitals on par with legendary works of art like
the Sistine Chapel."

Exercise! In her book, **Real Sex For Real Women**, Laura
Berman says, "A great sex life requires a healthy body and that

means more than just exercising regularly and eating a nutritious diet. A healthy body is the result of a fit mind, a fit lifestyle and a commitment to sexual health. Whatever your age or stage of life, a healthy body will help you achieve a satisfying sex life.

Our bodies shape our sexual experience and enjoyment, so taking care of our health should be one of our top priorities. Care for your body and watch your sex life soar."

The older we get the stiffer we become (not in a sexual context). Don't subscribe to the myth that you're "over the hill" sexually as you age.

Erotic massage builds intimacy and releases tension. Experiment with Erotic massage using heat activated massage oils. Explore each other's body. Get to know each other's sensitive spots. Caress gently.

Be an exhibitionist! At our age it's difficult, not necessary and not in our best interests, to be a contortionist. Emotions have a lot to do with your sexual satisfaction. Emotional sex is more rewarding then passive sex. You have to get into it. Full steam ahead! Emotional honesty, empathy, closeness, acceptance, flexibility and appreciation are all necessary and great indicators of a successful senior relationship.

Commit to each other by adhering to equal opportunity in giving and receiving. Take turns giving pleasure to each other. Be eager to please.

Elevate Grandma's desire by being entertaining and enthusiastic. Embrace her frequently and don't let your ego get in the way.

Establish the cozy habit of staying in physical contact when you get into bed at night. Stay close and savor the gentle physical contact as you drift off to sleep.

ED is not a name! When you can't rise to the occasion and are as useful as a '57' Chevy with rusted spark plugs, you may be suffering from erectile dysfunction. There is hope. Please consult your physician. Don't settle when you can get help and save the day.

ON THE SOFTER SIDE:

Here's the challenge for most of us: How do we get our partner to share our enthusiasm when it comes to having sex often? If you're like me, you wish you had the magic answer to that question!

For now, at least, forget about the challenge of simultaneous orgasms. Your challenge is to get her to want to have sex with you when you are up and ready!

Expectations! What do you expect from each other? I don't Expect anything from Grandma. Expectations lead to disappointment. It's a matter of trust.

I simply trust that she will be there for me when I need her. She also knows I'm there for her whatever her challenges may be.

Maybe you need to go back and revisit the letter "C" - engage in Conversation, share how much you care and get Connected if you feel disengaged.

Women need emotional connection to connect sexually. Just try to skip this step and you end up giving yourself pleasure without a partner's participation. Let's be honest. Self-pleasure is not nearly as much fun even if it does get the job done. Have realistic EXPECTATIONS. Lofty expectations foster disappointment.

The only person who can live up to your standards...is YOU! Don't demand the same level of performance from others.

Grandpa Does Grandma

The ABCs of Senior Sex

F

"Men are like Firemen...sex is an emergency and no matter what we're doing we can be ready in two minutes. Women, on the other hand, are like fire. They're very exciting, but the conditions have to be exactly right for it to occur."

Jerry Seinfeld

Foreplay can be fun. Find new ways to do the same thing. Try feathers, oils, lotions or potions. As women age, their vagina is typically slower to lubricate during foreplay. With that in mind, an extended period of non-genital lovemaking (kissing, stroking) should be part of your agenda. Fake a power outage at home. With no television to tempt you...no computer to occupy you...no phone to annoy you and with no furnace to heat you...you pretty much have no choice but to get out the candles, huddle around the fireplace and be romantic.

You don't have to reach the finish line. Just get in the race. If you have a fetish and it's part of your sexual routine, just do it. As long as there is fun and respect and no abuse, you are free to do whatever makes you happy. Use your imagination. In one of my focus groups, one man described dressing as a police officer while his wife played a criminal. Speaking of using your imagination, maybe you have conjured up some sexual fantasies. Sexual fantasies often include mental visualizations involving persons other than one's regular partner and may include sexual activities considered by many culturally inappropriate or unacceptable. Of course, our male fantasies usually involve sexually explicit material showcasing beautiful women who are sexually available and free. Our female partners are more likely to base their fantasies on sexual experiences that emphasize romance and intimacy. Alfred C. Kinsey, in his research, reported that fantasy accompanied masturbation for the majority (sixty-four percent} of females and virtually all males.

If you don't have a sexual fantasy, I invite you to join the crowd. I vote for anything that doesn't do any harm.

Remember the Yellow Pages ad, "Let your fingers do the walking?" Your fingers are a powerful sexual instrument for touching and stimulation. So, let your fingers do the talking. Focus on the relationship not sex.

"First, Foremost and Forever" should be your motto. Strive for focus as your ultimate goal. If focusing leads to sexual satisfaction, all the better. Following is an acronym for focus:

Fun Loving – **O**pen – **C**ommitted – **U**nselfish - **S**ensitive

On The Softer Side:

Now let's talk about the F word! As long as I brought it up, let's address it. The F word is fun. Senior sex doesn't have to be serious. In fact, sex never has to be serious.

It also doesn't have to be rigid or predictable. Let's be real. Women do not run on autopilot. Stoke their fire to get what you desire. Have fun.

When I was younger, women shared with me that flirting was a fun part of their dating experience. They recalled that courting combined with teasing created more interest in romance.

We need to step back and recall the days when sex was not part of dating, and when touch and flirting were the only acceptable behavior. (However, I'm not sure when that was!)

Of course, we're now seniors and recognize that we've been around the block thousands of times. However, that doesn't mean we can't go back to 'start' and bring fun back like in the "good old days."

If it worked then, who says it can't work now? Fun can lead to fulfillment. A little fun, a lot of fooling around and you're on you way to creating a fantastic day. That's worth a bit of effort. Would you not agree?

Grandpa Does Grandma

The ABCs of Senior Sex

G

*"Sexuality is not a leisure or part-time activity.
It is a way of being."*

Alexander Lowen

How about some golf course sex? Many seniors are living in golf communities. Groping in the moonlight kindles excitement. Why not pick a moonlit night and make love on the green of the hole nearest to you? Decide to either use your driver or simply stay with your putter. Obviously, your putter is an easier stroke. Some of us have longer putters than others.

Good hands are crucial to great sex. Use them to touch, fondle and stroke your partner. You may change your partners mood from "not now" to "yes". As with most good things, great sex is a combination of the right attitude, the right information and the right technology.

Want great sex? Great sex is Sight + Touch + Scent + Taste + Sound. In other words, see it, touch it, smell it, taste it and listen for the moans and groans and other telltale sounds.

If you can include those ingredients in your sexual encounters you will definitely be on you way to opening the gates of pleasure. At our age, we've finally figured out what we want and what we need for our sexual gratification. I guess that's because we've been practicing for a long time. Be gentle and give your all with gusto and without guilt.

After thousands of loving encounters with your partner, your sexual organs have or should have become best friends by now, with no secrets. Intimacy should have replaced privacy. In other words, nothing is held back. That probably gives us an advantage over the younger generation. I would like to believe it does. Be a generous spirit. Sometimes sex is delivered one way. That's OK. Your turn will come.

With all the talk about the environment, we should go green... Sexy play can be green and efficient as well. Showering together can save water, and if things get too steamy, you can take your amorous feelings to the bedroom but don't leave the shower running.

Organic cotton, hemp silk, bamboo and other renewable fibers can make ultra-sexy lingerie and underwear. Forget about crotch-less panties. We are a little too old for them.

As for condoms, they are essential in preventing sexually transmitted diseases if you are engaging in sex or still playing the dating game. Please note, however, that putting on a green condom will not automatically turn you into the Jolly Green Giant.

Let's not forget about good grooming and the gym? Do you work out on a regular basis? If not, why not? As we get older, we need to get our hearts pumping so we can keep on humping. Remember: the golden years are definitely hot! As for grooming, when you look in the mirror and begin to see those pesky hairs growing from your nose, ears, and elsewhere, it's time to get out the trimmer. No woman, young or old, wants to be intimate with an unkempt man.

ON THE SOFTER SIDE:

If I've heard it once, I've heard it over and over again. Women find it difficult to respond romantically when their partner is not sexually generous. Giving to your partner means satisfying her first.What a novel idea. Imagine focusing on her needs before focusing on your own.

Let your wife or your partner feel the pleasure of your attention, your touch, your tenderness and your whispers of love. Satisfy her first.

Give her your heart and she will return the pleasure. Be genuine. Put your needs aside and you will bring your relationship closer.

Grandpa Does Grandma

H

"Having sex is like playing bridge. If you don't have a good partner, you'd better have a good hand."

Woody Allen

A quick hand job will always be appreciated. Offer to help out by stroking yourself if your partner is working too hard. Senior genitals respond quickly to the right kind of gentle touch. If she works softer, you get harder. You are just a heartbeat away from a hard-on. Remember: If your erection lasts longer than four hours (we should be so lucky) call your doctor.

Hold hands whenever you can. Holding hands is often taken for granted as a way to express your feelings for your partner. It keeps you connected. It's really one of the simplest but most effective ways to show you care. No practice is necessary.

A good hug is one of the most pleasing things you can do to express your love for your mate. Everyone likes to be hugged! Give your partner hugs as often as you can throughout the day. Hugs can prevent the old "I have a headache" excuse. Hug your partner at the beginning of the day, the end of the day, during the day, and always after sex.

Humor is worth its weight in gold. Share some laughs when talking about your sexual wants and desires. While sex is often passionate, it's more often funny. For example, my father-in-law lived to be 90 and never lost his sense of humor. One evening, at a local restaurant, he went into the men's room. He often got a little confused as to where he was so I waited for him outside the door. As he exited he saw me and said with a grin on his face, "I just got a blow job." I looked at him in utter shock! "Are you kidding?" I asked. He quickly continued, "You know, that gizmo you put your hands under and it blows them dry." What a great sense of humor for a 90-year old Grandpa. Wouldn't you agree?

Take a closer look at your favorite positions and if you don't take yourselves too seriously, you'll both laugh out loud.

ON THE SOFTER SIDE:

You must have heart! A Country song said it best; "It takes a little rain to make love grow but it's heartache and pain that makes a real heart show."

Did you ever stop to realize that the first four letters in heart is hear? What is the one thing that a woman wants that can significantly contribute to her Happiness and have a significant impact on yours? She wants to be heard:

* Not while you're reading the Sunday sports section.

* Not when you're watching your favorite television show.

* Not when you're running out the door to meet your retired buddies for breakfast or a round of golf.

Women want to be heard when you can offer her your complete attention. When you can give your heart to her concerns, issues or ideas, that's when a woman knows she has your heart. It doesn't matter if what she has to say is considered unimportant to you. If it's important to her it had better be important to you. By now, I hope you recognize that a happy wife makes a happy life!

Do you insure harmony in your relationship? Want more hard-ons and hand jobs? Hear more with your heart and your wishes will come true.

Grandpa Does Grandma

The ABCs of Senior Sex

I

*"My love life is terrible. The last time I was inside a woman
was when I was inside the Statue of Liberty."*
Rodney Dangerfield

Intimacy! There is no substitute. In her book, **September
Songs,** author Maggie Scarf says..."For once again, intimacy
becomes a dominant priority: the marital partners must now move
closer and become more intimate as mates rather than focusing
on their careers or their departed or deprived offspring."

Intimacy means a lot more than simply having sex with a partner and is only one aspect of sexual closeness. It is the self-abandonment that accompanies intercourse. I believe very few couples achieve a true state of intimacy.

It's often been said that intimacy really means "into me see". You've got to share with your partner your most personal thoughts and desires.

Understanding your partner's wants and needs produces more satisfying results under the sheets. Personally, I'm not into mystery, I'm into full disclosure. I have no secrets from my wife. We fulfill each other's sexual needs.

Senior intimacy is the sharing of our souls and becoming so close and open to each other that we experience intense communication and understand each other on a deeper level. Intimacy is an attitude. Be clear about your intentions.

Senior sex is about innovation and improvisation. No need to play silly games. If you're in the mood for some sexual frivolity, regardless of the time of day or night, let your partner know by sending a clear message. If your partner is unavailable, why not take responsibility for engineering your own orgasm?

In the October 2008 issue of ***Esquire Magazine,*** the sexiest woman alive (according to Esquire), Halle Berry, said, "Don't wait, Initiate! Sex is not about frequency, it's about Intensity."

So apply what you've learned over the years. Note, however, that somebody once said, "For flavor, instant sex will never supercede the stuff you have to peel and cook." It is, admittedly, better than instant oatmeal.

On The Softer Side:

Individuality is a must in a relationship. Although it's important to function as a couple, it is equally important that each partner has a life of his/her own. In other words, the greater the strength of one's Individuality, the greater the growth of one's relationship. Exactly what do I mean? Grandma and I participate in the majority of activities together. Of course there are times when she does her thing and I do my thing, whatever that "thing" may be.

While we depend on each other, we are not dependent upon each other. Each of us maintains our separate careers as well as our own interests. We agree to support each other in whatever each of us chooses to do. We share many of the same values in life and give each other great value by being together.

Ever notice that partners tend to look alike when they've been together for a long time? Both of them may have silver hair, walk a bit slower, or talk a bit louder? I find it comforting to observe that as husbands and wives 'grow old together', they begin to show physical similarities.

That being said, focus groups indicated greater satisfaction in relationships takes place when each person maintains his/her Individuality.

Of course as we age, we adjust to one another's likes and dislikes, recognize our individual patterns of behavior and learn how to adjust to the way we differ. Compromise might be a better word. We come to terms with who we are and how we relate to our partner. I believe that independence is important in any relationship and is the same for seniors.

Personal integrity is a must. Each of us takes responsibility for doing what we say we will do.

Grandpa Does Grandma

The ABCs of Senior Sex

J

"If God was a woman she would have made sperm taste like chocolate."

Carrie Snow

Well, it's back! The new and updated edition of **"The Joy of Sex"** which was first released in 1972 has been revised by Susan Quilliam, a British sexologist, columnist and relationship counselor. The original version, written by a man I might add, remained on the New York Times best-seller list for an amazing 243 weeks.

According to a New York Times article dated December 18, 2008, the new version is written for women as well as men. It tackles an array of modern topics unheard of in the 1970s, like Internet pornography, AIDS and Viagra® and features photographs of a suitably buff 21st-century couple.

Here are some of the things that we know more about now than in the 70's according to Ms. Quilliam: "The arousal cycle, hormones, pheromones, the clitoris, the relevance of the nipples, how erections work, and aphrodisiacs."

The article goes on to say that..."in addition to the elusive G spot, women can also enjoy two other sexual pleasure points, should they be lucky enough to locate them: the A spot, deeper inside the vagina than the G spot; and the U spot, between the clitoris and the vagina."

While this latest edition of **The Joy of Sex** may update the sexual knowledge and mores of the younger generation, my question to Ms. Quilliam is simply, "Does the newer version contain information focused on the senior set who comprise a significant portion of our population?"

A good Jacuzzi® will work wonders for your sexual activity. Dim the lights. Burn some candles on the side of the tub. It will relax you and get you in the mood. Jets of warm water gently caressing your sensitive parts can be stimulating.

Jog briskly if you are physically fit. Jogging gets you out in the fresh air to enjoy the sounds, smells and scenery. If jogging doesn't turn you on, walking is also a wonderful exercise to promote a healthy lifestyle. How about a neighborhood stroll, hand in hand with your partner as a brisk start to your day, or a healthy after dinner activity?

How about some Jam? I'm not talking about Smuckers®. I'm not referring to putting jelly on your crackers.

I'm talking about Jam up and Jelly tight. That's all I have to say about this matter. Feel free to use your imagination.

ON THE SOFTER SIDE:

Joy is such a wonderful word. Choose to nurture a relationship that fills one's heart with joy, that is joyful and joyous and is worth all the effort, all the adjustments and can lead to a life that is sexually gratifying.

To experience this feeling, look at life with anticipation, gratitude, and satisfaction. I don't believe you can find joy by looking for it. It's an internal feeling of a life well lived.

It's what you feel inside when you feel great about yourself and want to share that feeling and inner peace with the person you love. Having sex when you feel great about yourself and your relationship is a satisfying combination for a wholesome partnership.

Grandpa Does Grandma

The ABCs of Senior Sex

K

"Kissing is a means of getting two people so close together that they can't see anything wrong with each other."
Rene Yasenek

The journey of romance begins with a lot of kissing. While most of the women in my focus groups agreed, it should be noted, however, the number one complaint from women in the groups was, "too much tongue."

Keep it simple. An anonymous woman once said, "Men are simple things. They can survive a whole weekend with only three things: beer, boxer shorts and batteries for the remote control."

While it's not my thing, kinky sex i.e. handcuffs, role-playing, whips and chains, master-servant, etc. can be exciting. Laughing, however, releases endorphins that instill feelings of happiness and well being.

Sex can be a kaleidoscope for discovering new feelings and excitement in each other's embraces and words. Have fun.

Purr like a kitten and show your appreciation and attraction to your spouse or partner. Powdered Dunkin' Donuts® are great after lovemaking and the white confectionary sugar or crumbs that fall on your bodies present new opportunities for pleasure... use your imagination!

ON THE SOFTER SIDE:

Kissing and kindness – A perfect combination! We can talk about the pleasures that come from kinky sex and engaging in very personal and unusual activity, however, never lose the value of being kind and loving and the intimacy of really luscious kissing. There is no limit to where or when.

Kiss the body parts where kissing can have a lingering effect. Light, tender, deep and penetrating, kisses can lead to deeper levels of closeness.

Let your kisses speak for your heart and the intensity of your love. The key to your sexual happiness to keep kindling the sparks of Love.

L

*"If you want to read about love and marriage,
you've got to buy two separate books."*

Alan King

A sexually gratifying senior relationship should be based on Luck! Love! and Lust! First, you must be lucky and hopefully, are still very much in love. Shower your loving relationship with lust. Lust is the fuel that keeps love alive and keeps the fire down below. I lust for Grandma every minute of every day.

When met with success, lubricate! lubricate! lubricate! As women get older their vagina is typically slower to lubricate during foreplay. Enjoy an extended period of non-genital lovemaking (kissing, stroking, etc.) as part of your agenda. Your partner's delayed responsiveness is physiologically similar to the longer time it takes for senior men to achieve an erection. Suffice it to say that at our age there can never be enough lubrication!

Bathe her body in luxurious, luscious, lovebird lotions. It's certain to get her libido going for a nighttime liaison. Whether you feel you need it or not, a little extra sliding and gliding can add something more to any in and out endeavor. The older your car gets the more oil you need. Remember to pack your favorite lubricant when traveling.

When having sex, laugh more, love more, lubricate more and leave the lights on. Seniors who recognize that their sexuality is a life long blessing enjoy a longer life!

Leave notes! I am constantly leaving notes for Grandma telling her how much I love her, miss her and want to devour her. I even put notes in her baggage when she travels. It keeps us close and in touch. By the way, she does the same for me.

ON THE SOFTER SIDE:

A relationship that is both lighthearted and loving has the best possible shot at keeping romance alive. As we age, we shouldn't take our spouse/partner or ourselves too seriously. Let your life together be free from the demands and stress of your youthful years. Embrace quiet moments.

Laugh a lot. Celebrate reaching this stage in your life as it continues to be well lived. Let's hear with hearts that do not edit and that strive to learn.

May your commitment to each other remain strong, your hearts remain entwined and may you bask in knowing you are loved beyond measure. Listen with your heart and talk openly with your partner.

Lighting is also important. Drape her red panties over the light to give a soft red glow to the room. If she doesn't have red panties, buy her a pair. After all, most brothels are in red for a reason.

Here are some examples of love notes we've written to each other.

"I'm almost home with the one person who makes my heart sing with joy." Signed: Mrs. P

Dear Heart, Thank you for the privilege and joy of being your wife. You are my sunshine, pleasure, re-assurance, love and tenderness. With all my heart, I truly love being Mrs. P

Seducing you still remains the best decision I've ever made. I continue to love and cherish you. Be safe. You are always on my mind. Love You...B

Being with you just feels right and being with you is my favorite place to be. B

Hi Honey, if you're putting on my nightshirt, knowing I'm on top of you makes me feel good. I love you...P

I love your parts because together they make up you. Love, Your main squeeze

I love you 24/7. You are definitely the wind beneath my wings. Loving you Always, Me

Let her know what you're thinking. For example, on July 16, 2005 Grandma and I renewed our marriage vows. I wrote the following;

I just want you to know:

I give you all my love freely because it's mine to give and I want you to have it.

When I think of your love, I smile from within my heart.

My passion for you is so warm and so intense

I would crawl naked over a bed of broken glass to get to you.

I just want you to know;

When I need your tenderness and support...you kiss my tears away.

Your unconditional love is my constant companion when days are long and cold.

Your love is my destiny when our lives grow old.

Our love will grow in all kinds of weather as long as you and I are together.

I just want you to know;

Maybe it's the fact that FATE played HER hand and our partnership was simply meant to be.

I will never take for granted the gift I've been given because I know that a soul mate is so very hard to find.

Maybe it's our never-ending friendship that makes our love so strong.

Now here we are in front of family and friends to continue our journey down the road to endless accomplishment, endless love and endless passion. So, close your eyes and hold my hand because...

I just want you to know;

I am your friend, your partner, your lover and soul mate for life.

I just want you to know:

I love you FIRST! FOREMOST! AND FOREVER!

Your husband in love and for life, Phil

M

*"We have reason to believe that man first walked
upright to free his hands for Masturbation."*

Lily Tomlin

Gin Rummy seems to be a favorite card game for seniors.
Both my mother and father played often. Of course they didn't
play together. She played with her women friends and he hung
out with his cronies. On one occasion I casually asked my father,
"What happens if you don't have a good hand?" Masturbation
means never having to explain to anyone. It's sort of like having
a winning hand every time. Masturbate together or engage in
mutual masturbation. You can learn something about the other's
arousal process. Sex in your sixties or seventies is not like a
Romance Novel.

I can't say enough about memories. We all have them. Create lasting and unforgettable memories and they will last a lifetime. Why not spend some quiet time with your partner and recall some of your favorites. Perhaps they will bring back some excitement from the past.

Here's something else to consider: the big M, menopause! If you have already experienced the ups and downs of this stage of your partner's life, congratulations! If not, read on.

It is not necessarily true that women lose interest in sex after menopause. In fact, most surveys of sexual behavior find an upswing in sexual frequency for women over sixty-five who have partners. Learn the facts about menopause. Recognize the symptoms that may affect your sexual functioning as a couple. Being supportive is critical, as symptoms will not last forever. Invest in your relationship now with care and understanding for long-term results. Tell your partner that you miss her even if it's only for one day.

Recently, while she was traveling, I wrote the following message to Grandma:

HONEY, I MISS YOU

I miss...beginning each day with you

I miss...having you next to me when I awake
I miss...hearing your alarm clock early in the morning
I miss...hearing the sound of your electric toothbrush
I miss...watching you shower in the morning

I miss...lying on the couch knowing you are nearby
I miss...sharing the excitement of our day's events
I miss...having ice cream together at bedtime

I miss...watching you undress each night
I miss...the bruises that mysteriously appear
I miss...the erection your naked body gives me
I miss...your wet kisses and loving embraces
I miss...exploring and gently caressing your body
I miss...holding you and the pleasure I receive
I miss...watching your body respond to my love
I miss...your hands exploring and caressing my body
I miss...my exhaustion after you hold me
I miss...your head on the pillow next to mine
I miss...our bedtime chatter
I miss...holding your hand as we get into bed
I miss...seeing your face as we drift into sleep
I miss...falling asleep next to the woman I love

I miss...ending each day with you

KNOW THAT I LOVE YOU...FIRST, FOREMOST and FOREVER!

ON THE SOFTER SIDE:

While I mentioned back rubs earlier, women in the focus groups shared that massage has an incredible way of stimulating a woman's desire for sex. It soothes, it relaxes and creates an atmosphere that brings a woman into a pleasurable state. In the January 2008 issue of The Economist it said, "...Around 40% of the lyrics of popular songs speak of romance, sexual relationships and sexual behavior. The Shakespearean theory, that music is at least one of the foods of love, has a strong claim to be true." Add music and it will be difficult for your partner to resist you or your sexual desire.

Don't think you have to be an expert or take lessons to give a great massage! Massage can be anything that involves touch – relaxing her shoulders, caressing her feet or soothing her scalp.

While watching television, why not consider sitting close together, your partner's head in your lap and begin to 'set the stage' for what you have in mind! That way, a little television watching will meet with her approval if you put down the remote and really focus on your partner. Whatever you do that is mutually pleasurable is worth time and effort.

To reiterate, it was a consistent message from the women who participated in the focus groups. Women want closeness, to feel connected and cared for as their foreplay. Obviously, this is quite different for us guys but a requirement if we are to be mutually satisfied.

So, don't pass off massage as unnecessary or insignificant! Let's do what we need to do to get the results we want. Keep your eye on the target.

N

"Women need a reason to have sex. Men just need a place."
Billy Crystal, Comedian/Actor

Never waste a hard on! Let's be honest. At our age we're lucky if we can still get hard. I'm not talking about hardening of the arteries. If your desires are met with resistance: Negotiate! Wouldn't you sooner have a nooner? Think about neatness. If you leave your underwear, socks, shirts, etc., thrown all over the bedroom, don't expect a candlelit sexual experience that night. Nobody likes a mess. Here's a thought: What might be the outcome if you were more considerate and more involved in household management? For example, from a woman's point of view, if you prepare dinner, do the laundry and go grocery shopping every once in awhile, she just might consider this "foreplay." Talk about a turn on for your spouse/partner when you begin to share responsibilities.

As far as need goes, keep in mind that generally a woman wants one man to satisfy her every need while a man wants his woman to satisfy his one need.

ON THE SOFTER SIDE:

That brings us to the importance of nurturing. Anything you can do that creates closeness is in your best interest and needs to be part of your agenda. So, you might be thinking, give me some examples.

How about unexpected pleasures – you know, like flowers! How about a loving note tucked in a place you are certain will be found? How about something special that isn't tied into a birthday, mother's day or your anniversary?

We all know that for the most part our lives are consistent and predictable. It doesn't have to be that way. To nurture your relationship is to give it your attention, to be deliberate and thoughtful beyond the normal day to day routine.

Nurturing can be non-verbal. I shared earlier about the importance of hugging and kissing.

Touch, smile, eye contact, a small pat on the butt are all non-verbal expressions that say, "I love you", "You're special", or signify connection. Women need and want connection.

They need your touch and acknowledgement frequently rather than occasionally.

What are you waiting for? Get what you want by giving your partner what she wants. It's not rocket science. It's simply the truth. Be a nurturer and offer non-verbal gestures and WHAM! Try it and get ready for some serious and perhaps unexpected returns.

Grandpa Does Grandma

"You are the sun, I am the moon
You are the words, I am the tune
Play me"

Neil Diamond

Be Oral - I'm not talking about Oral Roberts, Oral B toothbrushes or giving a speech in front of your peers. I'm talking about the Lick of Love! Put some lipstick on his dipstick. Guaranteed to turn Grandpa on at anytime and earn his appreciation as well. Don't forget to try some flavored massage oils. Oral sex is accepted as normal in today's society. It's a wonderful warm up to intercourse.

If you believe, as some do, that oral sex is good for your health, then a little fellatio each day may keep the doctor away. Comedian Carrie P. Snow said, "Oral sex works both ways." Don't be afraid to please your woman.

Isn't it interesting that many of the younger generation hold the belief that oral sex is not sex? What's that all about? That's a discussion for a later time. It will certainly make for interesting dialogue so why not have that conversation with your partner?

Keep an open mind. It's important in a constantly changing world that we stay open minded.

Are you willing to be open to new avenues of lovemaking? Are you willing to trust your partner to express what you want if you're not getting your needs met? If not? Why not?

All of us have obstacles to face and challenges to overcome. A loving relationship will provide the foundation to face any challenges, emotional as well as physical.

ON THE SOFTER SIDE:

Let's get serious for a moment. Seriously serious! How open are you in communicating with your partner? Women can be more easily romanced when their loved one or partner is open to sharing. Not Monday night football, the news, stock market report, who you bumped into at the library, or what's for dinner. This is not openness! It's more like a journalist reporting non-relevant happenings of the day. To be open is to share feelings, what moves you and what you're thinking about.

Aging is a process and as we get older and face our own mortality, we all experience doubts and concerns about life. We read about death and dying and we lose individuals close to us.

It's important that we share our feelings with each other as we approach the final chapter of our lives. Just as there is joy in life, there is also fear and uncertainty.

Be open to sharing. Be willing to both listen and learn from your partner.

Don't waste precious moments of enlightenment because you think it's unimportant.

Anything about you is important to share. Anything about your partner is important for you to know and accept.

If you want sexual openness, try verbal openness! You might be shocked at what happens. Let you partner know what you want and need.

Let her in and she'll let you in (no pun intended). Get it? Worth the effort, don't you think?

Grandpa Does Grandma

The ABCs of Senior Sex

P

"A penis is very sensitive, emotionally, that is,
and doesn't take criticism well."

Dr. Ruth Westheimer

Perfection and penetration should not be your ultimate goal! Don't always expect sex when everything is perfect. Penetrate whenever possible. Please understand that there is no such thing as perfect penetration. You don't have to be perfect, only perfect together. If you are unable to penetrate, pleasing yourself is always an option. At least you won't have to apologize to anyone. It's not the pace of your life that should concern you but rather the sudden stop at the end.

Think about phone sex. Sex over the phone is like guided masturbation. If it turns you on and your partner is not physically available, dial his/her number. There's no extra charge and for some, phone sex gets the job done.

As an added precaution, if you're playing around in several palaces of pleasure, be sure to wear a protective raincoat.

Don't underestimate the value of placing a pillow under Grandma's hips. Changing the angle of her hips may dramatically enhance your intercourse experience. According to Laura Berman, Ph.D., "For many women, lying in the missionary position with a few pillows under their buttocks provides the perfect pelvic tilt for G-spot stimulation and orgasm."

Let's not diminish the power of women. Recently I noticed this Internet Quote of the Day:

"Whatever you give a woman, she will make greater.

If you give her sperm, she'll give you a baby.

If you give her a house, she'll give you a home.

If you give her groceries, she'll give you a meal.

If you give her a smile, she'll give you her heart.

She multiplies and enlarges what is given to her.

So, if you give her any crap, be ready to receive a ton of shit!"

What more can I say?

ON THE SOFTER SIDE:

Does play have any role in your relationship? Are we too old to have fun? Have we simply forgotten that fun enhances a relationship? Do you ever go dancing, enjoy a matinee movie, hang out at a karaoke event or play cards and keep a running score?

Of course, there's always sexual playfulness. You can talk, tease and cajole when sex isn't possible.

For instance, when you're at a dinner party you can set the stage for when you get home and then get the candles ready and put the music on. I call it setting the stage for sexual success.

Don't forget the impact pampering can have on achieving sexual intimacy!

Are we too old to have breakfast in bed, to sleep on satin sheets or walk around naked? Are we too old to implement fresh ideas, new behaviors and experiment with new ideas and new sex toys?

When I asked women what they want, pampering was a top priority. Why not ask your spouse what she wants so you can pamper her for an entire day! "Tell me what YOU want and I will give it to you." I'm willing to bet that it gets you some timely but unexpected sex. Psychological intimacy - You have to really understand your partner to insure your sexual success. It's never too late.

Grandma and I are each other's #1 priority. It's one of the cornerstones of our successful relationship.

Grandpa Does Grandma

The ABCs of Senior Sex

"Sex is like art. Most of it's pretty bad and the good stuff is out of your range."

Scott Roeben

A "quickie" means sexual activity of any kind, not just intercourse. While it's not like hit-and-run sex with an eye on the clock or Zipper sex (oral sex performed hurriedly without removing your pants or while partially dressed), if you don't have time or energy for anything that requires effort, a quickie will get the job done. Most men can get an erection in the time it takes her to say..."How about a quickie?" Adding a lubricant speeds up the female process and will allow for quick penetration, if that's your goal.

Men have a quick sexual motor while women are more like a thorough bred racehorse. You've got to take them around the track a few times to get them warmed up.

If you are a Grandpa or Grandma who enjoys air travel and would like to become members of the "mile high club", you must be quick AND quiet.

ON THE SOFTER SIDE:

Women love quiet moments with the person they love.

We are constantly bombarded by sounds, ads, traffic and the hustle and bustle of everyday life. When we are preoccupied, focused on external conditions and overloaded, it's difficult to focus on intimate moments and sexual readiness. We must find ways to quiet our minds and focus on our lovemaking.

It's special to explore quiet, peaceful moments with the one you love and who loves you. Feeling peaceful and close is great in setting the stage for physical closeness. For example, walking along a beach, holding hands and listening to the sound of the ocean against the shore is a quiet moment. Can't get to a beach? Try walking in a nearby park or in the neighborhood after dark. With nothing but evening sounds, it's great to just be peaceful together. Caressing one another without speaking – non-verbal – is an example of quietness.

Come back from an evening walk, ditch the television and call it a day by retiring to bed early – not to sleep but to romp in a fantasy journey of sexual adventure! This is a perfect way to quiet the drama of the world outside your bedroom.

R

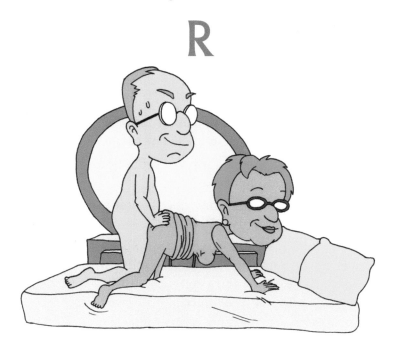

"Only the united beat of sex and heart together can create ecstasy."

Anais Nin, Philosopher

Risk is your personal travel agent on your journey toward sexual fulfillment. If you want to reach increased levels of intimacy and satisfaction, consider taking greater risks. Consider, that like any risk, you never know what the reward will be unless you take action. It's a risk/reward equation. The greater the risk, the greater the likelihood of reward.

Regret has no room in your life. You can't change past events. Enjoy what you have in the present moment. Katherine Mansfield said, "Regret is an appalling waste of energy and you can't build on it; it's good for only wallowing in it."

I hope you understand that eyes are the initial gateway to romance. There's no substitute for romancing your partner. You will get much better results. "Romance creates a context within which sexuality can be given more meaning. It focuses sexuality toward a loving purpose: The growth of intimacy.

It's the appreciation of two people who are celebrating the lucky coincidence that they found each other.

Without romance, sex is simply a seduction. With romance, sex becomes connected to love.

With romance, sex becomes about giving and not merely taking." (**LOVE** by Gregory J.P. Godek)

Romancing your partner can be as simple as leaving a note on the refrigerator, an unexpected hug, helping your partner clean the shower or bathtub or showing her you value her not only as bed partner but also a life partner.

It works *almost* every time. Not all romantic gestures will result in immediate sex but they certainly will make the goal much easier to reach. Build on the relationship you've built over the years to get the rocket out of your Pocket!

Many men want and appreciate role reversal. Grandma can seduce Grandpa and follow up her seduction with gentle stroking and gentle conversation.

ON THE SOFTER SIDE:

Remember Aretha Franklin's song, R.E.S.P.E.C.T? You can make huge progress in having your sexual desires met when your woman knows without a doubt that she has your respect. When she knows you admire her, appreciate her and hold her in high regard, you open the door to greater closeness that can lead to increased sexual frequency. I hope you're getting the picture without being hit over the head.

Speaking of head, want more? Show respect in every aspect of your relationship.

Respect how your partner thinks, what she feels and how she conducts herself and she will shower you with favors in return. Why wouldn't she?

Set realistic expectations of each other. Never become a victim of the "Happily Ever After" myth. Build your relationship skills. Become an expert at conflict resolution, communication, and sexual knowledge to insure a lifetime of loving.

As we age, we can easily succumb to the unrealistic pictures of youth. Believe it or not, we were all young once! Been there, done that.

Now is the time to appreciate and respect the distance we've traveled and the lessons we've learned.

Grandpa Does Grandma

The ABCs of Senior Sex

S

*"Sex, when you're married, is like going to a 7-11.
There's not as much variety, but at 3:00 in
the morning it's always there."*

Carol Leifer, Comedian

There's more to sex than four bare legs under a blanket. Sensitivity goes a long way! Our society is programmed for instant gratification or the need for speed. Sex is not only a tool of gratification and is also not necessarily gender driven. It's the language of the body designed to convey communication between hearts, minds, and souls. As seniors, it's important to be patient.

We have no need to rush until both partners are in the same place of desire and expectations.

Best selling author Maggie Scarf in her book, **September Song,** said..."the crucial thing to remember is that manual (or oral) stimulation of the male's organ by his partner is usually all that is necessary in order to promote and maintain his state of sexual arousal. In those instances where the female is unwilling to do this, the male may stimulate his own penis; but it is obviously more mutual and loving if this is an enterprise that involves both of them. In any event, it is *vital* to realize that manual or oral stimulation of the older male's penis may be viewed as the starter motor that will promote erotic sexual arousal and set the sexual encounter in motion."

In her book, **The Sex Bible**, author Susan Crain Bakos asks, "What's your signature sex move? Is it the way you kiss? The way you gently caress her vagina? Is it how you hold her hips when you thrust deeply? Discover it! Use it! Enjoy it!" If sizzling, spontaneous sex turns you on, make your intimate moments a sheet-clutching experience. If you have never slept or made love on Satin sheets, give them a try. A word of caution! Satin sheets can be slippery. You've got to be fast. It's challenging to have sex as your partner slides by.

As teenagers we were always trying to get into the box. As seniors, when it comes to sex, we need to get out of our comfort zone and think out of the box.

Don't be discouraged if your erection is not as large, straight, or hard as when you were in your youth. With a little help, it will continue to be sturdy and reliable. No need to play taps for Mr. Wiggly quite yet.

If you discover that you have difficulty moving around in bed or some other place of choice, why not consider sit down sex? Simply sit in a chair and have your partner sit on your manhood.

What about shower sex? Sex in the shower is steamy and slippery. Grandpa can shampoo grandma from behind by gently washing her breasts, torso and inner thighs. In return, Grandma can lather Grandpa up using a warm washcloth. Just remember his testicles are like breakable eggs, so be gentle. If there's room, she can also kneel down and give grandpa some warm and wet oral sex.

Having sex in the shower with your partner is like one stop shopping. It's like a two-for-one bargain. You get exciting sex and clean sex all at the same time. Not only do you share a nice relaxing hot shower but also enjoy some good hot sex and get to clean each off without any mess as part of the experience. For us men, we don't have to wait for our wife/partner to get finished.

Sex is 90% mental and 10% genital. The National Council on Aging did a study and found..."sex didn't stop because of a few gray hairs."

Additional findings showed that..."71% of men in their 60s, 57% in their 70s and 27% over 80 engaged in some kind of sexual activity at least once a month. For women, 51% in their 60s, 30% in their 70s and 18% in their 80s were active in the same period.

As seniors stay healthy longer, and surgery and drugs improve our sexual performance and drive, these numbers could actually increase." Aren't we lucky?

When there's snow on the roof, it doesn't mean the fire has gone out in the furnace. George Burns once said, "Sex after 90 is like shooting pool with a rope."

Hey, senior sex is one thing but any kind of sex after 90 would be incredible. It is an experience I expect to enjoy.

Separate sex from love. Your love may be taken for granted (I hope that's not the case) but at our age sex is taken anytime we can get it.

It's my personal belief that loss of memory as we age is, in part, due to lack of sex. Burlesque queen Mae West said; "Sex is an emotion in motion."

For seniors who are a bit slower to arouse, sex toys might be helpful to get the motor running. Sex toys are a great way to start sexual stimulation. Choose sex toys from reputable companies and ones that don't have chemicals. Keep your toys clean, in a convenient place, with batteries charged and you'll be off to a great party.

For silicone, rubber or cyber skin sex toys, use water- based lubricants.

ON THE SOFTER SIDE:

It's easy to be set in our ways at this stage of our relationship as we continue to enjoy a full life. Each of us has our own routine. I have mine and my wife has hers. Does this mean it has to remain the same way forever or is there room for diversion, change of pace and newness?

Does your bedroom have to be the only appropriate place for a sexual encounter?

Does late at night have to be the only suitable time for lovemaking? Change can be fun, open new doors, create new possibilities and provide new sexual adventures. It's not too late to be flexible. Let's not let past patterns dictate the only way to live our lives.

Why not bring spontaneity into your sexual behavior? Go for the quickie before joining friends for dinner and wink at one another all night long. Forget enjoying a traditional dinner. Instead, have some dinnertime sex and then afterward go out for pizza.

Sit in the last row of the movie theater and stroke one another during the sexy scenes. Why not? Let's be honest. Most of us can remember how as teenagers, we "made-out" when movie theaters had balconies. So, why give that up as seniors? Who will know? You can finish off what you started when you get home. Create your own reality instead of simply watching reality television.

What does it take to satisfy Grandma besides an orgasm? What does it take for Grandma to feel secure? It's so simple that there is no excuse for any man not to have a loving relationship with his partner. Just love her.

A great relationship exists where listening is a priority, where having fun together is the norm, and where a woman knows that her husband is her best friend. They feel connected beyond just sharing the same roof.

In my first book, "Kiss Yourself Hello! From a Life of Business to the Business of Life", I shared with my reader that the only thing my first wife and I had in common was that we got married on the same day.

What an unfortunate circumstance to be in when life can be so precious, productive and loving. I'm not suggesting that you "bag" an unfulfilling relationship. I am saying that men need to provide their spouses the security they deserve. By creating a loving environment, filled with trust, openness and generosity, you will not only enjoy satisfaction in all aspects of your life but also in your sexual adventures.

Space is very important to seniors. We've lived long and productive lives and every now and then we may desire some time for ourselves. For whatever reason, I'm not sure. For me, I would be happy to spend 24/7 with the woman I love...Grandma.

Grandpa Does Grandma

The ABCs of Senior Sex

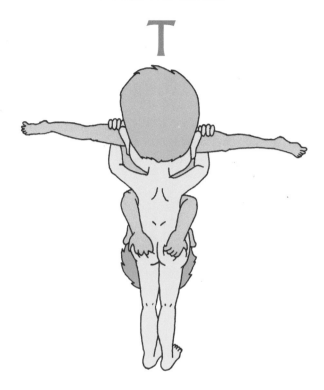

"Before marriage, a man declares he would lay down his life to serve you; after marriage, he won't even lay down his newspaper to talk to you."
Helen Rowland

We may strive for tight and taut although at our age it is unlikely. I work out regularly. I do my best keep my 70-year old body in shape for my senior sexcapades. Grandma does the same. While our bodies are less than perfect, we are nonetheless, in excellent shape for our age. This definitely enhances our sexuality.

While being thoughtful is nice, your hands, your penis, her vagina, her breasts or your tongue may be more useful. Your tongue is a powerful sexual instrument. French kissing is the more traditional use for your tongue.

However, in the 21st century, oral sex is a well-recognized part of sexual activity and Dr. Ruth Westheimer said in her book, **Sex for Dummies** that "vulvas have a special place in their hearts for a warm, moist tongue." And don't be afraid to tickle his pickle. Your tongue can play an important role too.

Don't overlook thankfulness. Thankfulness separates the younger generation from the senior generation. You've heard the saying, "eat and run." Thanking your spouse or partner for sex is wonderful expression even though the sex was free. Show each other where you like to be touched and the type of touching that pleases you. Lightly is the most thrilling. Be imaginative in how and where you touch your partner. It's our way of saying "I love you, I appreciate you and I'm so glad you're part of my life."

You have to trust your partner implicitly and without reservation. A trusting relationship is one that will continue to grow stronger each day. Without trust your relationship will wilt, wither, and die.

Most of you may believe that as you reach the status of senior citizen, your relationship has been built on love. I disagree! While you can love your partner, if you don't trust him/her, your relationship won't work. If your relationship is not working it's a safe bet your sex life isn't doing well either.

Set the tone for your sexual encounters and be tolerant of your partner. Women are thankful for tolerance and want an understanding partner. You will discover the twinkle in her eyes and feel her tremble at your touch.

If the Kama Sutra is to complicated or isn't working for you, investigate Tantric sex.

It uses breathing techniques to intensify intimacy as well as orgasms. Tantric sex connects the physical with spiritual enlightenment.

ON THE SOFTER SIDE:

Touch, tenderness and teasing. Sound terrific? I know I've hit the letter 'T' previously, only with different words. Women love to be touched; they love to be treated lovingly and engaged in playful behavior.

If you can't meet these needs then you need to examine your actions and make necessary changes. Remember the song, "Try A Little Tenderness"? Believe me, it works.

Listen today and get the benefit of being a great listener later. Be tender and have your gentle behavior reciprocated. Engage in emotional and intellectual togetherness.

Tease each other. Flirt and create romantic moments. These ideas are a "no brainer." They are Romance 101 in any guidebook.

So, begin to bring more touch, tenderness and teasing into your relationship if you want more sex. That, for most of us, should be a big motivator!

Spending time together will get you more of the results you want.

Grandpa Does Grandma

"Love at first sight is easy to understand. It's when two people have been looking at each other for a lifetime that it becomes a miracle."
Amy Bloom

U CAN DO IT TO YOURSELF - You won't have to apologize to anyone. Why not take a private moment to discover your own sexuality as you like it? Utilize the handy gadget whenever possible. You can play with yourself or play with a partner. Either way you might get the same result. Never worry about underperforming. The fact that we're able to perform at all is worth noting. Senior sex is not utilitarian. It's utopia.

ON THE SOFTER SIDE:

Appreciate your Uniqueness - We are a team in everything we do together. As individuals, each of us allows the other to grow.

We listen to each other and are patient and understanding of each other.

I must admit, however, that patience has not been one of my strong points although I am constantly working on it. We appreciate our commonality while at the same time acknowledging our differences. No judgments!

Is your love unconditional? Are you committed to understanding especially when you and your partner differ in points of view?

We all bring beliefs into every encounter. This is how we think something should be. This is what you could have done. If you would have handled this differently, think of the outcome instead of what actually happened. Hey, get real. We all relate to our lives and situations based on where we are at any given time. When we assume instead of seeking the truth or make decisions based on past experiences, we may wander into uncharted sexual territory. That is why love must be unconditional.

It doesn't matter what mistakes are made or what YOU think. Live life as it unfolds. Unconditional love has no limitations, no judgments and no right or wrong.

When you choose understanding, when you are sincere in seeking truth and make love your number one priority, your life will be satisfying, your relationship fulfilling and your sex fantastic. Give what is needed and receive what you want. Not a bad way to approach life. Agree?

V

"If a man can't stand to see his lover use a vibrator, my advice to the woman is; keep the vibrator and recycle the man."
Betty Dodson, Ph.D., Sexologist/Author

Viagra®, Vitamins, and Vibrators! As seniors we have become part of the **"V"** Generation. Be sure to take your daily complement of vitamins. I've experimented with all types. I've purchased vitamins from local merchants, signed up for vitamins customized for my own body, and I'm now taking encapsulated fruits and vegetables. Do they work? I feel great so I guess the answer is, "Yes."

I've heard rumors that Viagra® is responsible for nursing home orgies. Personally, I can't say much about Viagra®. Up to this point I've not found the necessity to use it. My brain and my genitals are still talking to each other. So far, so good!

That being said, if you need some help in that area, I'm told that Viagra® will get you up for the task at hand *IF* your heart is healthy enough to have sex.

As for vibrators, according to Treehugger.com, the Durex Global Sex Survey says, "43% of Americans have used a vibrator. Worldwide, more than 20% of adults have used a vibrator." Let's be honest, vibrators, dildos, anal beads, etc., can be thrilling and fulfilling. Be sure to invest (wisely) in a travel vibrator. For example, The Pocket Rocket. Buy a rechargeable one or you can use your own rechargeable batteries. Test it for noise and output strength before you spend your money. You can purchase the Rabbit made popular by the hit TV show "Sex and the City" or you can purchase Flipper the Dipper at your local adult sex shop. If you're a female with all the standard equipment, your choice of vibrator can be a matter of widely varying taste.

Several come to mind; Rabbit vibrators have a long, phallic, rotating shaft that penetrates the vagina while simultaneously a clitoral stimulator vibrates independently. G-spot vibrators are built with a curved tip and a long shaft.

Once inserted, a woman can reach her G-spot on the upper wall of her vagina. How about a remote controlled vibrator? It fits into your panties w/o wires. Just press the remote for instant pleasure. WOW!

While vibrators seem more common for women, let's not forget about the men.

Our best choice is probably an electric or battery powered vibrator that comes with a cup-shaped attachment. It's designed to surround the head of your penis and transmit vibrations directly to the penal glands. As an aside, if you have a pacemaker and you're using a vibrator, make sure they are not on the same frequency. While you may double your pleasure you may also increase your pain. Value the intimacy of your relationship. Remember when sex had nothing to do with love, fidelity, commitment and responsibility? As seniors, we are time tested Veterans of the Sexual Revolution.

ON THE SOFTER SIDE:

After focusing on my 'V' words, I quickly discovered women had their own view of how best to describe their 'V'. Their V was for vulnerability. Women cry easily, share feelings willingly and empathize passionately. Women who are willing to be vulnerable recognize that it fosters intimacy. The challenge is getting their man to be as open as they are. Get it?

I'm telling you that vulnerability leads to intimacy. More openness = more intimacy. Do I make myself clear?

My newly discovered 'V' word is NOT vagina – it's visit. That's right: visit!

I read somewhere that just asking your wife/partner when you want to have sex may not be as romantic as, "Can I visit with you!" Imagine that! At first, I thought that asking Grandma if I could visit was weird. Asking to visit instead of simply asking for sex seemed kind of kinky.

Asking if you can visit, however, actually sounds romantic. "I would love to Visit with you tonight." Or, "Let's go to bed early so we can have time for a visit! It gives your partner some heads up that you are looking forward to some sex later in the day or night.

If visiting is not your cup of tea, some other approaches may be: Shall we shake the sheets? Would you like to do the horizontal twist and shout? Do you want to take a trip to the land down under? Or simply, Can my snake play in your grass? Visiting is still working for me. It all sounds better than, "Do you want to get laid?"

Hey, if another approach works better, by all means go for it. If you're not getting anywhere with the way you're expressing your desires now, you can always test this expression to see if it gets the results you want.

"If wrinkles must be written upon our brows, let them not be written upon the heart. The spirit should never grow old."
John Kenneth Galbraith

Workout! Most of us should have more physical exercise. But, I'm not only talking about working out at your local health club. There are also many internal exercises that men and women can do to insure better sex. Pilates and certain types of Yoga pay attention to our sexual muscles. I've read that the Chinese have a tradition of energy exercises, mostly for men that build sexual health and enjoyment.

Vigorous sex is also a great workout. When in doubt...Just DO it! Have sex! Use it or lose it. Better to wear it out rather than rust it out. Watch your partner undress. Ask him/her to undress slowly, with emotion. It can also be a turn-on.

Count your Wealth. I'm not referring to financial wealth but rather the Wealth of memories you have with your partner.

Recognizing you've been together for many years, you have accumulated endless memories guaranteed to bring you closer as you share past experiences.

Don't waste your time together. It's one of life's most precious gifts. Use it wisely.

Gratifying sex is not the only thing to smile about. How about the wealth of natural gas we've accumulated as we've become seniors? Granted, it's not the kind of gas you can use in your car.

ON THE SOFTER SIDE:

Did you ever stop to consider that you and your partner bear witness to each other's lives? You may have spent years together. You have built a life, weathered storms, raised children (perhaps), dealt with grandchildren, lived through economic ups and downs, adjusted to different upbringing, endured loss and continue to face and adjust to the reality of growing old. You can never be closer to any one individual as you are to the person you share your life with every single day.

You witness what gives your partner pleasure, what causes discomfort, how each of you react to life as it presents itself and everything in between.

My wife often says, "I'm a witness to your life," when she sees me in an emotional or vulnerable situation.

Consider it an honor to bear witness to one another's life and hold what you learn in high esteem. Allow for truth, respect your differences and appreciate the gift of loving another human being.

Being in awe of your partner as you witness her life can foster grandiose sexual openness.

X

"Turn off the TV, turn on your partner."

Unknown

X-rated movies may work for you! If they turn you on...turn them on. As we mature past our 40's and 50's, from holding hands to candlelit nights, a glass of wine, a walk in the woods, instant gratification slowly diminishes. A professionally crafted X-rated movie may work for you. It will help re-energize your sexual desires. Let's face it. We're hard-wired for sex. Two good-looking professional actors in a sexual romp could be stimulating. Some of them are quite good. Actually, I'm not sure exactly what they're good for except to show you how to feel totally inadequate and how to make a mess during your sexual adventure. Let's get real.

How many orgasms can a senior have during a two-hour movie? I'd be thankful for one, wouldn't you?

If X-rated floats your boat why not take a cruise on the love boat? Just because it's not for me, doesn't mean it's not the perfect booster shot for you.

ON THE SOFTER SIDE:

Nothing can ruin a relationship faster than having Xpectations. When you give, do so with a full and unconditional heart.

Give because it makes you feel good. Give because it's the right thing to do. If you xpect something and it doesn't work out, it's only because none of us can control the outcome of any gesture. Be loving simply because you love your partner. Be a great listener simply because you want to connect and show respect.

Be sensitive and nurturing simply because it will bring you closer to your loved one. Offer these gestures because of love and not because you expect something in return. Disappointment usually results from unfulfilled expectations. The more you do to strengthen your relationship, the better the outcome will be for both of you.

Nothing speaks louder than love and love is what makes both of you feel great about yourselves, each other and your individual sexuality.

Give a little and maybe you'll get a little! Give a lot and you just might get back more than even you can handle. A word of caution! There are no guarantees.

Y

"Say NO to late night snacks; say YES to late night sex."
Phil Parker

Getting a yes is always music to a man's ears. When your partner agrees to your advances, you are well on your way to sexual success. Remember that late night snacks put pounds on while aggressive late night sex can take pounds off. Try it; you might like it!

Consider doing yoga. The benefits of yoga are great and help people young and old stay fit, flexible and focused. It involves all parts of your body and is great for increasing your stamina. It's available to all ages.

Anyone, especially seniors, who want to stay healthy, strong and sexy, will surely enjoy the rewards they reap from doing yoga. Be sure to consult your physician before signing up for classes.

The hippies of the 60's were the flower children that were going to change the world.

In our younger years we may have been sexually experienced and sexually functional. That doesn't mean, however, that we were sexually educated.

As seniors, each time we have fulfilling sex we should look at each other and yell, "Yippie!" as an affirmation of what we've learned and how wonderful, true intimacy can be at any age.

ON THE SOFTER SIDE:

The simple truth is we are getting older. We are in or at least approaching the twilight of our years. It's true. We are aging citizens living in a land that revolves around Youth. Everything today is about anti-aging. The answer for us is to remain young at heart. Live with a great attitude.

Feel proud of what you've accomplished, where you've been and continue to live a productive life. In many ways, sex is wasted on the young.

They are less experienced, hop from one bed to another and don't stay long enough to build the closeness that we, today's seniors, have achieved. I'll admit, however, they do have more energy!

What we need to do to enjoy a quality of life as we age is simply to remain Young At Heart.

Stop yearning to recover your younger years. It's not a possibility. Continue to make the most of your sexuality and sexual opportunities during your senior years.

Enjoy the fruits of your commitment to one another. Experiment. Feel free. Lead with your heart. Love as you never have before. Stay young at heart during all your intimate moments. Go for quality sex, not quantity!

Grandpa Does Grandma

The ABCs of Senior Sex

Z

First you forget names, then you forget faces, then you forget to pull your zipper up and then you forget to pull your zipper down."
Leo Rosenberg

Zip up or zip down? That is the question. I suppose it depends on who is doing the zipping. If you're fortunate enough to have your partner give you some unexpected but always welcomed action, I guess you can zip down in preparation. Remember to zip up when you're finished. Zero in on her erogenous zones. By now, I'm certain you know where they are.

Practice the art of Zen. The art of Zen is achieving mindfulness or being involved in the present. What human activity can be more "mindful" than blissful sex?

There is no distraction, hopefully no anxiety, only the excitement and exultation of two loving bodies touching each other during an intimate moment in life's journey.

ON THE SOFTER SIDE:

I hope you are enjoying every moment of every day. Whether you're cuddling on the couch, sitting in the back row at the movies playfully stroking each other, going for a walk along the beach, doing dishes together or just relaxing, may you exhibit a zest for life.

As we embrace our twilight years, it becomes more urgent to make the most of the time we have. Zest for life is about keeping love alive, sex fulfilling and bringing out the best in each other and your relationship.

Grandpa Does Grandma

Grandpa Does Grandma

"HAPPILY EVER AFTER"

EIGHT ATTRIBUTES OF POSITIVE ENDURING MARRIAGES

An ability to change and tolerate change

An ability to live with the unchangeable

An assumption of permanence

Trust

A balance of dependencies

An enjoyment of each other

A shared history that is cherished

Luck

From "Married People"
By Marilyn Klagsbrun

Grandpa Does Grandma

The ABCs of Senior Sex

(And, finally) On the Serious Side
DEATH and DYING

Every time a senior citizen dies,
It's more than another human being,
Another valuable pair of eyes is lost,
And all that they have seen.

The many changes in our lifestyles,
Stories of how it used to be.
Our wise advice is going silent,
Along with ethics and morality.

One at a time they're leaving us,
So are values and integrity.
The world now lives far away
From how it used to be.

These elders knew what they were saying,
Their words were kept at any cost.
Marriages worked and survived,
Just another thing we've lost.

Pride was taken in their jobs,
Almost everyone seemed to care.
They prayed and ate together,
The yesteryears are no longer there.

The very last fiber is about to snap.
Which holds together our family ties.
Who will tell us of how life used to be,
If the last senior citizen dies?

B.G. Wetherby

Grandpa Does Grandma

The ABCs of Senior Sex

SUGGESTED WEB SITES FOR YOUR EDUCATION AND ENRICHMENT

www.GrandpaDoesGrandma.com

www.bermansexualhealth.com

www.aarp.org

www.redhotmamas.org

www.loveologyuniversity.com

www.patlove.com

www.ellentwhite.com

www.seniorjournal.com

www.amazon.com (Look under Sex for Seniors)

www.advancedseniorsolutions.com

www.health.discovery.com

www.seniorcitizensdailynews.com

www.drruth.com

www.sagehealthnetwork.com

www.mayoclinic.com (Look under senior health)

www.goofyfootpress.com

www.hisandherhealth.com

Grandpa Does Grandma

The ABCs of Senior Sex

SUGGESTED READING

Men, Love and Sex and *Eat This, Not That* by David Zinczenko

Sex For One by Betty Dodson, Ph.D. Sexologist

Regaining the Power of Youth by Kenneth H. Cooper, M.D.

The Great Lover Playbook by Lou Paget

September Songs, The Good News About Marriage in the Later Years and *Intimate Partners* by Maggie Scarf

The Longevity Revolution: The Benefits and Challenges of Living a Long Life by Dr. Robert N. Butler

Women On Top by Nancy Friday

Idiots Guide to Tantric Sex by Dr. Judy Kuriansky

Guide To Getting It On *(goofy foot press)*

Ordering Information:

Grandpa Does Grandma:
The ABCs of Senior Sex

Single copies $14.95 US / $19.95 CDN
3 or more copies $12.95 US / $15.95 CDN

Shipping and Handling:
$3.00 per single copy/ US
$6.00 per single copy/ CDN
Call Toll free: 1-888-489-9393
Visit: www.GrandpaDoesGrandma.com
OR
Mail you order to:
Phil Parker
P.O. Box 725586
Atlanta, GA 31139

Please allow 4 weeks for delivery.

About The Author

Phil Parker is a professional speaker/author and senior citizen who has enlightened audiences worldwide with his creative and humorous insights. His topics include but are not limited to: *Life Is A Business, So Let's Get Busy; Change is Inevitable Except From A Vending Machine* and of course *Grandpa Does Grandma: The ABCs of Senior Sex*.

He lives with Grandma in Atlanta, Georgia.

For information on his availability
Call toll free: 1-888-489-9393
Visit Phil at www.PhilParker.com or at
www.GrandpaDoesGrandma.com
Email: Grandpa@GrandpaDoesGrandma.com

Write to: Phil Parker
P.O. Box 725586
Atlanta, GA. 31139

CPSIA information can be obtained
at www.ICGtesting.com
Printed in the USA
BVHW020014010222
627317BV00001B/1

* 9 7 8 0 9 7 2 4 0 6 1 6 1 *